POWWOW

Summit Free Public Library

Photographs and text by **GEORGE ANCONA**

HARCOURT, INC.

Orlando   Austin   New York   San Diego   Toronto   London

Requests for permission to make copies of any
part of the work should be mailed to the following
address: Permissions Department, Harcourt, Inc.,
6277 Sea Harbor Drive, Orlando, Florida 32887-6777.

Library of Congress Cataloging-in-Publication Data
Ancona, George.
Powwow/photographs and text
by George Ancona.—1st ed.
p. cm.
Summary: A photo essay on the pan-Indian celebration
called a powwow, this particular one being held
on the Crow Reservation in Montana.
ISBN 0-15-263268-9 (hc)   ISBN 0-15-263269-7 (pb)
1. Crow Fair, Crow Agency, Mont.—Juvenile
literature. 2. Powwows—Juvenile literature.
[1. Powwows. 2. Indians of North America—Rites
and ceremonies.] I. Title.
E99.C92A53   1993   92-15912
394.2′68′089975—dc20

Designed by Camilla Filancia

U T S R Q   (pb)   3 9547 00357 6217

Printed in Singapore

My gratitude goes out to the gracious hospitality of the people at Crow Fair for making this book possible. In particular to John Pretty On Top, a member of the Crow Tribal Council, who offered his knowledge and gave permission to photograph the participants and events of the powwow. Also to the family of Anthony Joe Standing Rock for their cooperation. And last, but not least, to Tim Peck, my editor on this book, whose knowledge and enthusiasm made this a most enlightening and exciting project to share.

For Corina

Introduction

One story told is that the word *powwow* came from French explorers who misunderstood the native word describing a gathering of people coming together to trade. Its true origin may never be known.

Originally, some dances were performed before warriors left the village to hunt, raid, or do battle, and after they returned to celebrate their successes. Other dances were also performed as religious ceremonies and to honor individuals or to initiate members of different tribal organizations, called societies. But not all tribes gathered to dance with others since many were enemies.

Nowadays differences are set aside. Crow, Lakota, Cheyenne, Cree, Ojibwa, and many other native peoples from all over North America come together to celebrate and reaffirm their shared heritage and traditions as Native Americans. Old war-society dances have blended to become a general dance style, and other styles have also been rediscovered to create the four main types of dancing seen at today's powwows: Traditional, Fancy, Grass, and Jingle-dress.

Many dancers' clothes reflect a particular tribe in design and decoration, but there are others whose clothes are a combination of different traditions. Some dancers wear the floral patterns of the Woodlands, and some wear the geometric patterns of the Plains, and some wear a mixture of styles. Some even decorate their dance clothes with modern sequins, materials, and dyes instead of glass beads and porcupine quills, but the basic patterns can still be seen.

Today powwows take place all over the United States and Canada. They are a unique pan-Indian celebration of Native American culture.

For a week now, cars, trucks, vans, and trailers have been rolling across the vast, hot prairie. It is time for Crow Fair, the biggest powwow in North America. Every summer, people from all over the United States and Canada travel to the Crow Reservation in Montana to attend Crow Fair. Lakota, Ojibwa, Cheyenne, Crow, Cree, Blackfeet, Fox, and more come from cities, towns, and other reservations to celebrate their shared heritage as Native Americans.

One by one, slender wooden poles arc through the air, and their ends are joined together to form the frame of another tepee. The men wrap white canvas around the skeleton, and a new lodge takes its place among the seemingly endless clusters of Crow dwellings. Some of the poles are left with greenery on top to flutter in the breeze.

In the past, the tepee was used by Plains Indians because it is sturdy, portable, and easy to set up and take down. It was a practical home they could take with them as they followed the seasonal migrations of the buffalo herds and other game. Today, tepees are a symbol of cultural heritage and are used for special occasions.

At Crow Fair, some people build bowers next to their tepees to have a shady spot for the cooking, eating, and visiting that will go on during the powwow.

The powwow is a time for renewing old friendships and making new ones. Children play together and ride bareback among the tents and tepees. They ride so easily, they seem to have been born on horses.

Anthony Standing Rock plays with a friend inside the empty dancing arbor that will soon be filled with dancers, singers, and spectators. He and his family have traveled far to attend this year's Crow Fair.

A parade signals the beginning of the powwow. First comes the honor guard made up of men who have served in the U.S. military. A warrior's bravery has always been valued by Native Americans. Those who have fought in America's wars are honored as they would have been centuries ago.

Riding behind the honor guard are leaders wearing warbonnets. Dressed in traditional clothing, men, women, and children follow, riding horses adorned with decorated saddles, bright blankets, and colorful breastplates and headstalls.

The parade moves along the road that circles the encampment and the dancing arbor.

After the parade, the voice of the master of ceremonies comes from the loudspeakers in the dancing arbor, summoning the singers and dancers. The dancing is about to begin.

Anthony races back to his family's camp to change into his dance clothes. He puts on a fringed deerskin breechcloth, leggings, a beaded vest, gauntlets, a knife sheath, moccasins, and a feather bustle (a semicircular display of eagle feathers tied to his lower back). Anthony's eyes can hardly be seen under the eagle and hawk feathers of his dog-soldier headdress. In his right hand he carries a bow and arrow, and in his left, a quiver.

These are the clothes of a Traditional dancer, which Anthony's mother and father worked long hours to make for him. Just applying beads to one square inch of material can take up to an hour. Anthony is very proud of his dance clothes.

Not everyone in Anthony's family dances at every powwow, and when not dancing, family members often share parts of their dance clothes with one another. A young dancer's clothes are often made up of items that have been passed down from one dancer to the next.

Under the shade of the dancing arbor, the drums assemble. At a powwow, a group of singers who sing as they beat a rhythm in unison on a large drum is called a *drum*.

These singers must know many kinds of songs for all the different dances, honorings, and special events that can take place. The drums become the pulse and heartbeat of the powwow. The master of ceremonies will call upon each of the twenty-eight drums that are attending the fair to take turns singing for the dancers.

Good drums can become very popular. Fans and spectators cluster around their favorites to record the songs. They will use these recordings later to practice their own dancing and singing.

During breaks, the drum itself is covered with a blanket as a sign of respect.

Outside the dancing arbor, the dancers gather in a kaleidoscope of feathers, beadwork, fringe, and face paint. Inside the arbor, spectators find seats and wait for the dancing to begin. A feeling of excitement and anticipation fills the air.

Everyone waits for the opening ceremony, called the Grand Entry, that signals the beginning of the dancing. The dancers form into groups according to the style of dance they will perform. Men, women, and children of all ages are dressed in one of the four dance categories: Traditional, Fancy, Grass, and Jingle-dress.

In the crowd, Anthony and his friends wait for their signal to enter the arbor.

As the loudspeakers burst with the sound of the drum selected for the Grand Entry, the honor guards hoist their flags and rifles. With a toe-heel step in time with the drum, they enter the empty space of the dancing arbor. Slowly they move around the arbor to the beat of the song.

Young women, called princesses, follow the honor guard. They proudly wear sashes proclaiming the area or group they represent. Each princess will hold her position for one year, then a new princess will be chosen.

"*Uta hey, uta hey!* Let's go, let's go!" shouts the master of ceremonies. His voice blends with the beat of the drum, the high voices of the singers, and the bells on the legs and feet of the dancers.

The princesses and honored guests are followed by the dramatic and stately Traditional dancers. Then, in a dazzling burst of color and movement, the Fancy dancers enter. The men's brightly colored regalia sparkles in the sunlight, and the women's fringed shawls flutter in the air. Then come the Grass dancers, weaving and shaking their long fringe. A tinkling fills the air as the Jingle-dress dancers gracefully enter the arbor. And finally, the children join the adults as they step, jump, weave, and spin to the music of the drum.

Moving slowly in a clockwise direction, five hundred dancers fill the grassy area. Traditional women dancers step lightly in a reserved manner while Fancy men dancers spin and whirl about them. From under the moccasins of the dancers, the scent of crushed grass mingles with the dry Montana dust that fills the air. At powwows there are some dances that are just for men and some dances that are just for women. But during the intertribal dance that follows the Grand Entry, everyone participates.

The sun is hot, and beads of perspiration trickle down painted faces. When the drum stops, the dancers stop. They leave the arbor, panting and catching their breath.

After the intertribal, the individual groups of dancers will display their skills. Like most large pow-wows today, Crow Fair offers prizes to the best dancers from each category: Traditional, Fancy, Grass, and Jingle-dress.

The first to dance are the Traditional men. Years ago, Native Americans lived close to nature, and this is reflected in the Traditional dancer's clothes. Feathers from eagles and other birds, porcupine quills, shells, horsehair, and the skins from deer, ermine, otter, wolf, and other animals are worn.

Traditional men wear a single bustle tied to the lower back. Some wear feathered bonnets, while others wear a warrior's hair-piece, called a roach, made from deer tail, porcupine, or horsehair with one or two feathers in the center. They carry decorated weapons, feather fans, staffs, or other items that hold special meaning for the dancer. Some dancers also paint their faces in designs that reflect a personal vision. These designs can come from a dream or an important experience the dancer has had.

The Native Americans who lived on the Plains survived by hunting. The animals' flesh was used for food, skins became clothing, sinew became thread for sewing, and antlers and bones were made into tools. It was believed that the only way animals could be hunted and killed was if they understood the hunter's need and willingly gave themselves up to him. And if their gift of life was not respected, the next time the hunter went out, the animals would hide. Because of this relationship and dependence on nature, dancers honor the spirits of the animals that are part of their dance clothes. They treat their clothes with respect and care.

With the coming of Europeans, new items were introduced to Native Americans through trade. Cloth of cotton or wool, called trade cloth, was made into shirts and leggings. Ribbons appeared, and colorful glass beads replaced dyed porcupine quills for decorating moccasins, vests, and other items. Metal bells were tied to the dancers' legs to accent the rhythm of the drum.

The dance of the Traditional men is dramatic. Some dancers imitate the movements of animals or birds. Others move in a crouched position as if tracking or hunting. The dancers echo a past when men relied on their skills as hunters and warriors to survive.

There is a change in mood when the Traditional women dancers enter the dancing arbor. With their backs straight and heads held high, they move in a regal manner. Each dancer carries a beautiful shawl draped over one arm, and in the opposite hand she holds an eagle-feather fan. Their dance steps have a slight dip that makes the fringe on their clothes sway gently to the rhythm of the drum. The strength and beauty of their movement fills the arbor.

Like those of the Traditional men, the women's clothes reflect a closeness to nature. Dresses are often made from the skins of animals such as deer and elk and are decorated with porcupine quills, cowrie shells, and elk teeth. But the influence of trade with Europeans can also be seen. Cotton and wool trade cloth can be used for dresses. Machine-made fringe decorates shawls, and glass beads glint from dress yokes, sleeves, moccasins, and leggings. A woman's leggings, unlike a man's, cover only her calf, not the entire leg.

After the Traditional dancers come the Fancy dancers. The men are the first to perform. To the driving rhythm of a fast drum, brilliant regalia explodes with color as the dancers spin and twist, moving around the dance arbor. Young men like this energetic style of dancing. Strength and endurance are needed to be able to perform the quick steps and fast turns that are part of Fancy men's dancing.

The Fancy dancer's clothes are based on Traditional style. What makes them stand out from the Traditional dancer's is color—lots and lots of vibrant color. Chemical dyes, metallic beads, flashy sequins, and ribbons create a spectacular display. And instead of a single bustle, the Fancy man wears two: one at his lower back and another at his shoulders.

Equally beautiful are the Fancy women dancers. They wear their shawls over their shoulders while holding the ends in their hands. Some dance with their hands on their hips, elbows extended. Others stretch out their arms, spreading their fancy shawls while they jump, whirl, and step to the fast beat of the drum. The long fringe on their shawls, which is never permitted to touch the ground, comes alive. At times, the dancers look like exotic birds in flight.

This style of dancing, sometimes called Fancy Shawl, is popular with young women and girls. It requires nimbleness to perform the fast footwork, spins, and leaps. And just like the men, Fancy women dancers dazzle the spectators with their ribbons, colorful feathers, and sequins that give the traditional patterns a modern look.

At the end of each dance, the dancers leave the arbor hot, tired, and thirsty. Outside the arbor is a fairway with concession stands selling all kinds of food and drink. The dancers can rest and cool off with a soda pop or ice cream. And it's always fun to share some fry bread or a hot dog with friends.

There are also stands where dancers can buy materials for their dance clothes. Skins, feathers, beads, bells, shawls, and many other items are for sale. Tape recordings of the different drums, T-shirts, and other souvenirs can also be found along the fairway.

A new drum is selected, and as the singers' voices fill the air, the Grass dancers begin to weave and bend to the music. This is a man's dance based on old war-society dances of the northern plains. In this fast stepping style, the dancer almost appears to be falling off balance, then catching himself just in time.

Different from both the Traditional and Fancy dancers' clothes, the Grass dancers' regalia consists of long yarn fringe and ribbons that hang from their shoulders, waist, and legs. These dancers wear no bustle. On their heads, each wears a beaded headband and a warrior's head roach. Each dancer carries an eagle-feather fan and other items like small hoops, whips, and wands. As the dancers weave and dip, their long fringe seems to wave like the grasses of the prairie swaying in the wind.

In contrast to the fast-paced, tee-tering style of the Grass dancers is the gentle grace of the Jingle-dress dancers.

The Jingle-dress dance is very old. One story tells about an Ojibwa shaman, a medicine man, whose daughter was very sick.

One night the shaman dreamed of a dress that had a shell hanging from it for every day of the year. In his dream, a voice told him that if his daughter danced in this dress, she would get well. When he awoke, the shaman made the dress and asked his daughter to dance in it. She did, and she was cured.

The dance almost disappeared, but it has had a revival among young dancers. Today, instead of shells, the tin tops from chewing-tobacco cans are rolled into cones and sewn on the dress. During the dance, the cones strike one another, producing a pleasant tinkling sound.

In one hand the dancer carries an eagle-feather fan, while the other rests on her hip. Her steps seem effortless, blending graceful footwork and gentle hops that cause the cones to jingle in time with the drumbeats.

In addition to the dancing, the powwow is a place where traditions such as generosity and honoring are kept alive and passed on from one generation to the next.

At one point, a young woman is honored by her relatives for her skill as a Jingle-dress dancer. She stands alone in the arbor; then as the drumbeats shake the ground and the singers' voices fill the air, she begins to dance. She is so graceful, she seems to float across the grass. As she dances, her relatives lay personal items like a prized shawl on the ground for her to dance on. By stepping on the shawl and moving away, the young woman shows that the honor she is receiving is far greater than material possessions.

After she has danced on the shawl, anyone in the crowd who is in need of it, or of any other item that has been placed on the ground, may come and take it. This is a type of *giveaway* where a person is honored and, in turn, shares the honor with others through gifts. For many Native Americans, wealth is shown by a person's ability to help and share with others.

Another special honor is the introduction ceremony. A Navajo family from the Southwest has come many miles to introduce their little girl to the dance community. Her brother is a Fancy dancer, and he, too, has gone through the introduction ceremony that is about to be held for her.

After the two grandmothers offer a prayer in their native language, the family begins dancing alone around the arbor. As they dance, people step forward and shake hands with the father and give him small gifts of money. The line dancing behind the family grows as more people step forward to shake hands and join the procession, showing their support for the little girl and her family. This is the dance community's way of recognizing and welcoming the little girl as a powwow dancer.

Children of all ages participate at powwows, learning about their heritage. And just like the adults, they can compete for prizes in the four dance categories: Traditional, Fancy, Grass, and Jingle-dress.

Even the youngest, the tiny tots, have a special place of their own at the powwow.

When Anthony dances, he says he feels like a warrior. He hopes to win a prize for his dancing at this year's Crow Fair. But prize or no prize, Anthony wouldn't miss the fun of the powwow for anything in the world.